snapshot·picture·library

POLAR ANIMALS

snapshot·picture·library

POLAR ANIMALS

FOG CITY PRESS

Published by Fog City Press,
a division of Weldon Owen Inc.
814 Montgomery Street
San Francisco, CA 94133
www.weldonowen.com

WELDON OWEN GROUP
Chief Executive Officer John Owen
Chief Financial Officer Simon Fraser

WELDON OWEN INC.
President, Chief Executive Officer Terry Newell
Vice President, International Sales Stuart Laurence
Vice President, Sales & Marketing Amy Kaneko
Vice President, Publisher Roger Shaw
Vice President, Creative Director Gaye Allen
Managing Editor Karen Penzes
Assistant Editor Sonia Vallabh
Art Director Kelly Booth
Designer Andreas Schueller
Design Assistant Justin Hallman
Production Director Chris Hemesath
Production Manager Michelle Duggan
Sales Manager Emily Bartle
Color Manager Teri Bell

Text Maria Behan
Picture Research Brandi Valenza

A WELDON OWEN PRODUCTION
© 2007 Weldon Owen Inc.

Library of Congress Control Number: 2007936042

ISBN-13: 978-1-74089-654-2
ISBN-10: 1-74089-654-8

10 9 8 7 6 5 4 3 2 1

Color separations by Sang Choy International, Singapore.
Printed by Tien Wah Press in Singapore.

The north and south poles are located at the top and bottom of our planet. These two polar regions are both very cold, and spend most of the year covered by ice and snow.

When people imagine the poles and the areas around them, they usually imagine an empty, freezing land. But as you'll see, polar places are home to lots of amazing animals, many of which can't be found anywhere else!

Baby harp seals, like many of the animals that live in polar places, are white like the snow.

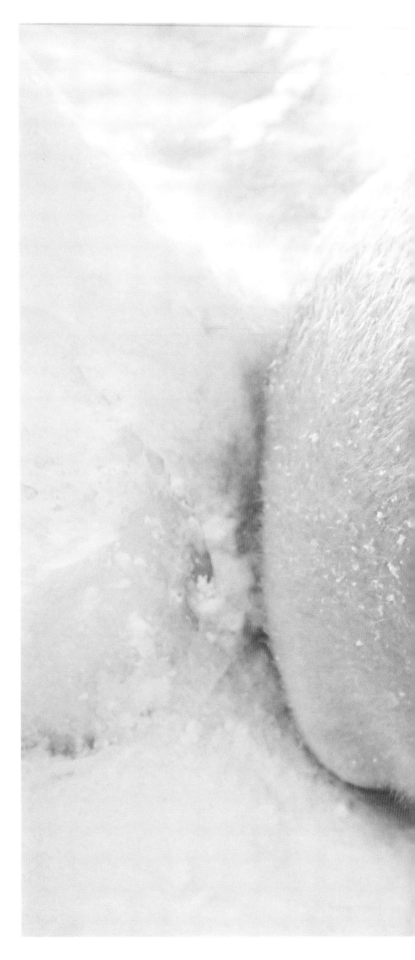

When seals grow up, they're a darker color. They stand out more in the snow—but they blend in well when they're swimming!

Seals are great swimmers, with back flippers that are made for the water. On land, they pull themselves along with their front flippers.

Like all seals, polar seals love soaking up the sun. They enjoy it when they can—since there aren't too many sunny days near the poles!

Elephant seals are the biggest
seals of all. Can you guess how
they got their name?

One way to tell the difference between a seal and a walrus is to look at their mouths. Walruses have two big teeth, called tusks.

These walruses look like they're trying to hide their tusks. But they can't fool you, can they?

Seals and walruses can be quite large, but the biggest polar animals are the whales that live in and visit that cold, cold water.

Like all whales, this beluga has a hole in the top of his head. Believe it or not, that blowhole is what he breathes out of!

Polar bears and seals don't have blowholes. But they're pretty good at holding their breath while hunting underwater.

Polar bears do most of their hunting underwater. When they're on land, they tend to sleep and take it easy.

Polar bears' big paws act like snowshoes, helping them get around on snow and ice.

Wolverines, wolves, and some special kinds of dogs live in polar places, too.

Dogs like
samoyeds
and huskies
help people
by pulling
their sleds
over the snow.

Arctic foxes have thick fur that keeps them warm. They even have fur on the bottoms of their feet!

Their fur changes color with the seasons. In the winter, it is white to match the snow; and in the summer, it is brown-gray.

Like arctic foxes, ermines and snowshoe hares change color with the seasons. But cute arctic ground squirrels look the same all year long.

Unlike most
other deer,
both male and
female reindeer
have antlers.

Caribou is another word for the reindeer that live in North America. Elk live there, too—as well as in parts of Asia.

Different kinds
of sheep and
oxen also live
in chilly polar
places. Some
have long fur to
keep them cozy.

Birds like terns, geese, and albatrosses live in polar regions, too.

Like many of the other animals
that live in snowy places, lots
of polar birds are white.

Not all polar birds blend in. With their black wings and bright orange feet, these puffins would certainly stand out in the snow!

Puffins' beaks aren't just colorful. They can hold a few small fish at once—very handy for bringing food to their babies.

But emperor penguins might be the best bird parents of all. They take turns watching over their babies, which are brown until they grow up.

This fancy penguin isn't wearing a hat! It's a rockhopper, which lives at the southern tip of South America.

It's cold in the snow. Let's stay
warm by playing together!

Ermine
Arctic regions of Europe, Asia, and North America

Elephant Seal
Pacific coast of North America, far southern hemisphere

Antarctic Fur Seal
Antarctic waters and South Georgia

Siberian Husky
Sled dog in far northern cultures

Elephant Seal
Pacific coast of North America, far southern hemisphere

Polar Bear
The Arctic

Emperor Penguins
Antarctica

Walrus
Arctic seas of northern hemisphere

Polar Bear
The Arctic

Harp Seal
Coasts of North Atlantic Ocean

Walrus
Arctic seas of northern hemisphere

Polar Bear
The Arctic

Elephant Seal Pup
Pacific coast of North America, far southern hemisphere

Harbor Seal
Coastal waters of northern hemisphere

Polar Bear
The Arctic

Sea Lion
Coasts of both northern and southern hemispheres

Walrus
Arctic seas of northern hemisphere

Polar Bear
The Arctic

Antarctic Fur Seal
Antarctic waters and South Georgia

Walrus
Arctic seas of northern hemisphere

Polar Bear
The Arctic

Weddell Seal
Antarctica, far southern hemisphere

Beluga
Arctic and sub-arctic waters of northern hemisphere

Wolverine
Isolated regions of far northern hemisphere

Baltic Ringed Seal
Arctic Ocean

Southern Right Whale
Waters of the far southern hemisphere

Arctic Wolf
Northern Canada and northern Greenland

Antarctic Fur Seal
Antarctic waters and South Georgia

Humpback Whale
Waters worldwide

Arctic Wolf
Northern Canda and northern Greenland

Weddell Seal
Antarctica, far southern hemisphere

Beluga
Arctic and sub-arctic waters of northern hemisphere

Samoyed
Sled dog in far northern cultures

Siberian Husky
Sled dog in far northern cultures

 Reindeer
Northernmost Europe, Asia, and North America

 Atlantic Puffin
Northern Europe, northern North America, Iceland

 Siberian Husky
Sled dog in far northern cultures

 Reindeer
Northernmost Europe, Asia, and North America

 Atlantic Puffin
Northern Europe, northern North America, Iceland

 Arctic Fox
Arctic regions of the northern hemisphere

 Musk Ox
Northernmost Canada, Greenland, and Alaska

 Atlantic Puffin
Northern Europe, northern North America, Iceland

 Arctic Fox
Arctic regions of the northern hemisphere

 Stone's Sheep
Northern Canada and Siberia

 Emperor Penguin
Antarctica

 Arctic Fox
Arctic regions of the northern hemisphere

 Dall Sheep
Northern Canada and Siberia

 Emperor Penguin
Antarctica

 Arctic Fox
Arctic regions of the northern hemisphere

 Arctic Tern
Far nothern Europe, Asia, and North America

 Emperor Penguin
Antarctica

 Ermine
Arctic regions of Europe, Asia, and North America

 Snow Goose
Northern Canada and Siberia

 Southern Rockhopper Penguin
Falkland Islands, Argentina, Chile

 Arctic Hare
Northernmost Canada, Greenland, and Alaska

 Albatross
Southern hemisphere

 Adelie Penguin
Antarctica and nearby islands

 Arctic Ground Squirrel
Canada and Siberia

 Snowy Owl
Northernmost Canada, Europe, and Asia

 Gentoo Penguin
Sub-Antarctic Islands

 Reindeer
Northernmost Europe, Asia, and North America

 Ptarmigan
Northernmost Europe, Asia, and North America

 Chinstrap Penguin
Antarctica and islands of far southern hemisphere

 Reindeer
Northernmost Europe, Asia, and North America

 Atlantic Puffin
Northern Europe, northern North America, Iceland

ACKNOWLEDGMENTS

Weldon Owen would like to thank the following people for their assistance in the production of this book: Diana Heom, Ashley Martinez, Danielle Parker, Lucie Parker, Phil Paulick, and Erin Zaunbrecher.